OH, BROTHER!

Family Jokes
Compiled by Charles Keller
Illustrated by Edward Frascino

Prentice-Hall, Inc./Englewood Cliffs, New Jersey

Copyright © 1982 by Charles Keller
Illustrations copyright © 1982 by Edward Frascino
All rights reserved. No part of this book may be
reproduced in any form, or by any means,
except for the inclusion of brief quotations in a review,
without permission in writing from the publisher.
Printed in the United States of America   · J
Prentice-Hall International, Inc., London
Prentice-Hall of Australia, Pty. Ltd., North Sydney
Prentice-Hall of Canada, Ltd., Toronto
Prentice-Hall of India Private Ltd., New Delhi
Prentice-Hall of Japan, Inc., Tokyo
Prentice-Hall of Southeast Asia Pte. Ltd., Singapore
Whitehall Books Limited, Wellington, New Zealand

10 9 8 7 6 5 4 3 2 1

Library of Congress Cataloging in Publication Data
Keller, Charles. Oh, brother, and other family jokes.
Summary: A collection of jokes about members of the family.
1. Family—Anecdotes, facetiae, satire, etc.
2. Wit and humor, Juvenile. [1. Family—Anecdotes,
facetiae, satire, etc. 2. Jokes]
I. Frascino, Edward, ill. II. Title.
PN6231.F3K4   1982   818'.5402   81-19890
ISBN 0-13-633305-2   AACR2

For Barbara, Betsy, Carol, and Ronnie

My brother writes TGIF on all his shoes. I wonder what that means?
It means, "Toes go in first."

Don't talk with your mouth full.
When I talk with it empty you say, "Go on with your dinner."

Does your mother yell at you a lot?
No, by the time she's through hollering at my brothers and sisters, she usually has a sore throat.

Who is your favorite author?
My father.
Your father? What does he write?
Checks.

My son just got his driver's license.
How long did it take him to drive?
About two and one-half cars.

How did you do on your first day of school?
Not too good, I guess. I have to go back tomorrow.

My uncle invented a foolproof burglar alarm. He could
 have made a fortune.
What happened to it?
Somebody stole it.

THAT'S THE FOURTH TIME YOU'VE GONE BACK FOR CAKE AND ICE CREAM. DOESN'T IT EMBARRASS YOU?
WHY SHOULD IT? I KEEP TELLING THEM IT'S FOR YOU.

Stop reaching for your food. Haven't you got a
   tongue?
Yes, but my arm's longer.

If you had two ice cream cones and your little brother
   asked you for one, how many would you have?
Two.

I have an uncle in Alaska.
Nome?
Of course I know him.
I mean Nome in Alaska.
Sure, I'd know him anywhere.

What time is it?
I don't know, but it's not five o'clock yet.
How do you know?
Because my mother said I must be home at
 five o'clock and I'm not home yet.

My mother has the worst memory of anyone I know.
Forgets everything, hmm?
No, remembers everything.

Mom, can I go out tonight?
With so much homework?
No, with my boyfriend.

My sister went on a garlic diet.
What did she lose?
Ten pounds and all her friends.

If you take one more piece of cake, you'll burst.
Pass the cake and get out of the way.

Dad, can I have two dollars?
Don't you know the value of a dollar?
Of course, that's why I'm asking for two.

My grandfather fought in the Second World War and
 my father fought in Vietnam and my uncle fought in
 Korea.
Gee, can't your folks get along with anybody?

I won a prize in school today. The teacher asked how many legs a hippopotamus had and I said three.
How could you win a prize with that answer?
I came the closest.

Your report card is terrible! Are you a slow learner?
I'm not a slow learner. I'm just a fast forgetter.

My parents don't understand me. Do yours?
My parents? I don't think they've ever met you.

REMEMBER, A FOOL AND HIS MONEY ARE SOON PARTED.
I LIKE YOU FOR PARTING WITH IT JUST THE SAME, UNCLE HARRY.

WAITER, PLEASE WRAP UP THIS LEFTOVER STEAK FOR MY DOG.
OH, BOY! WE'RE GOING TO GET A DOG.

How do you always get so dirty?
Well, Mom, I'm a lot closer to the ground than you
   are.

I'd like to go a full day without scolding you.
You have my permission, Mom.

Did your father help you with this problem?
No, I got it wrong by myself.

What did your father say when he fell off the ladder?
Should I leave out the dirty words?
Certainly.
Nothing.

IF YOU DON'T STOP PLAYING THAT GUITAR SOON I'LL GO OUT OF MY MIND!
DAD, I STOPPED PLAYING AN HOUR AGO.

Don't whistle while you study.
I'm not studying, just whistling.

Son, I'm worried about your being at the bottom of your class in school.
Don't worry about it, Dad. They teach the same things at both ends.

One more bite like that, and you'll leave the table.
One more bite like that, and I'll be finished.

Son, I want you to have all the things I didn't have when I was a boy.
Oh, you mean like all A's on my report card?

21

You usually talk on the phone for an hour, but you only talked for half an hour tonight. What happened?
Wrong number.

It's time to get up. The birds were up a long time ago. If I had to sleep in a nest of sticks and straws, I'd get up early too.

When I was a little boy, I always ate my spinach.
Did you like it?
Of course I did.
Good, then you can have mine.

Didn't you promise me you'd get good marks in school?
Yes, Mother.
And didn't I promise you no spending money if you didn't?
Yes, but since I broke my promise, you don't have to keep yours.

How come you're wearing your brother's raincoat?
I don't want to get his new sweater wet.

Dad, are you good at remembering faces?
Why, yes.
That's good. I just broke your shaving mirror.

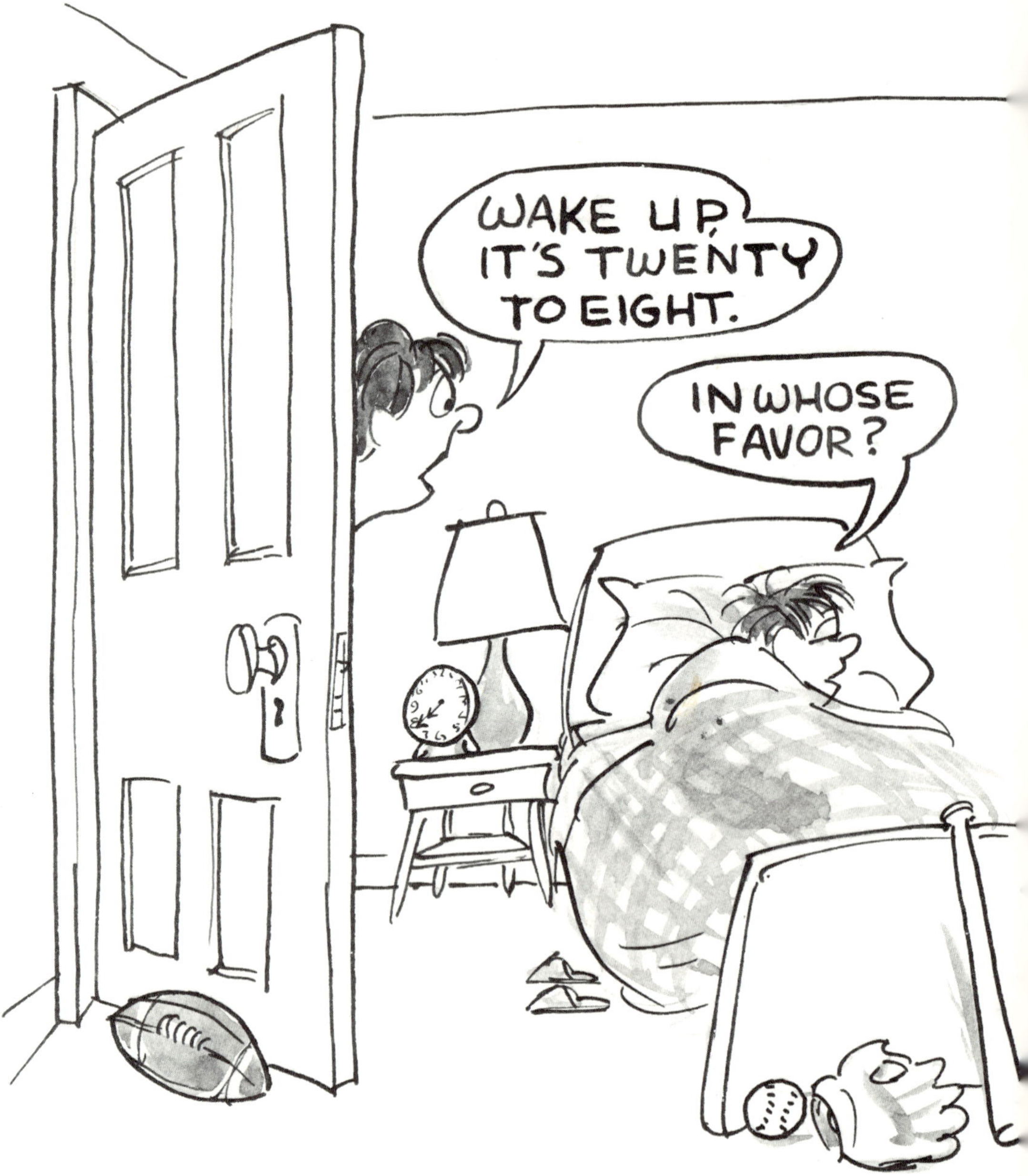
WAKE UP, IT'S TWENTY TO EIGHT.
IN WHOSE FAVOR?

Where are you going, Mom?
To the shopping center. They're having a giant sale.
Does that mean that I'll have to give up my room
   when you bring him home?

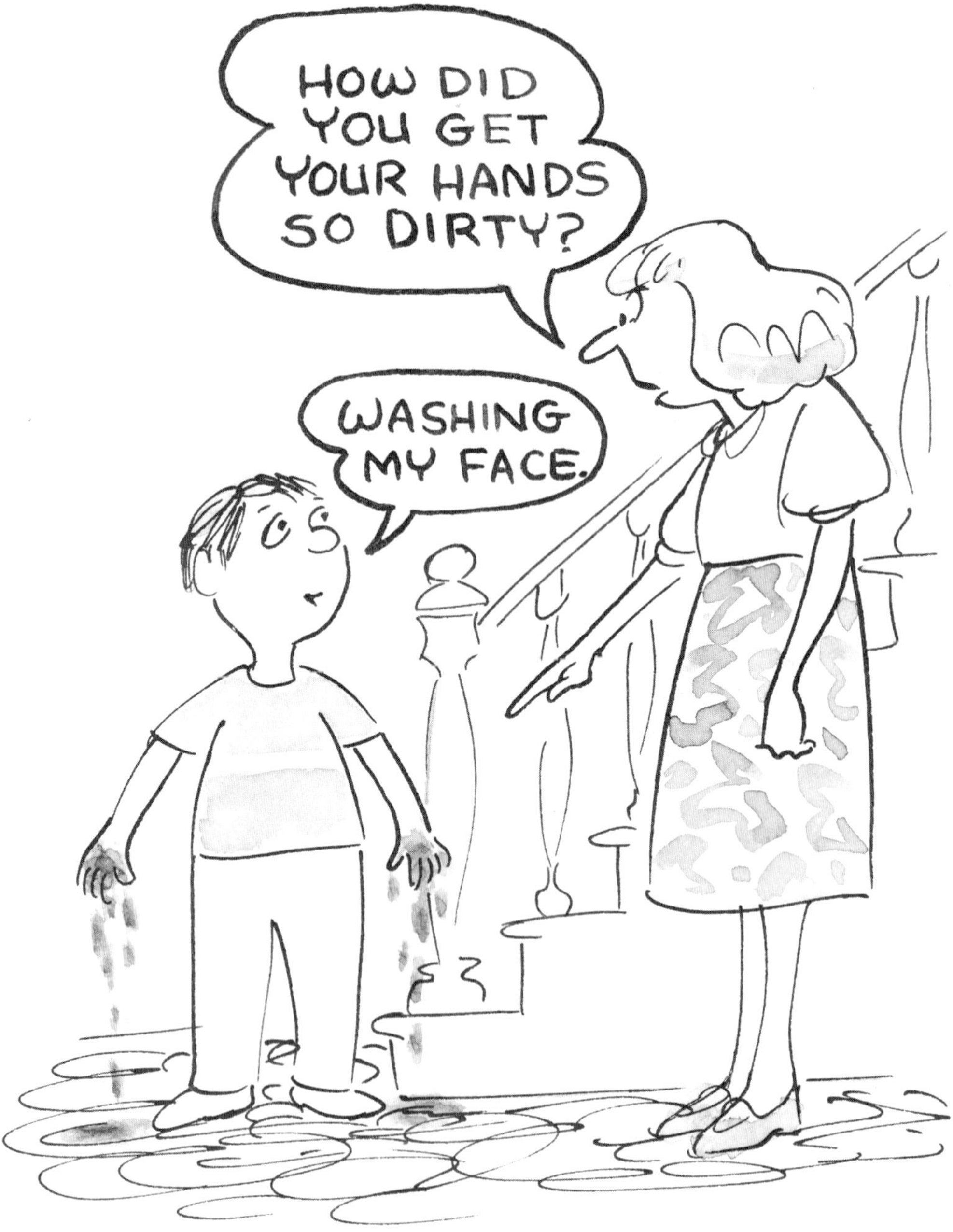
HOW DID YOU GET YOUR HANDS SO DIRTY?
WASHING MY FACE.

Things are a lot different from when I was a boy. My son has a color TV, a stereo, a home movie outfit, and a telephone in his room.
How do you punish him?
I have to send him to my room.

Did you put on a clean pair of socks every day this week?
Yes, I did. But now I can't get my shoes on.

How many controls do you have on your TV set?
Four—my father, my mother, and my two brothers.

Mom, I found a wristwatch.
Are you sure it was lost?
Of course it was lost. I saw the man looking for it.

I've been helping you, Mommy.
What have you been doing?
I licked all the stamps so they'll be ready to put on
   your letters.

Hey, Mom, the baby finally ate all his oatmeal.
I wonder why he suddenly liked it?
I told him it was mud.

Mom, I'm glad you named me Billy.
Why?
Because that's what all the kids in school call me.

Today's your birthday. Do you remember on
   what day you were born?
No, I was too young.

Son, when Lincoln was your age he was out splitting rails.
Yes, I know, Dad. And when he was your age he was president.

Ma, what was the name of the last station?
Don't bother me. I don't know.
That's too bad, because little brother got off there.

How come you get into so much more trouble than any other boy?
Well, it's probably because you make me get up much earlier.

How come you got such a poor mark in history?
They keep asking me questions about things that happened before I was born.

COOKIES
MOLASS
I DO EVERYTHING AROUND THIS HOUSE.
THAT'S NOT TRUE. I MAKE THE MESS.

BEFORE YOU COME IN HERE, ARE YOUR FEET DIRTY?
YES, BUT I HAVE MY SHOES ON.

Why is your report card so poor?
I can't help it. I don't sit next to any smart students.

Did you give the fifty cents to charity?
No, I thought I'd give it to the ice cream man and let him give it to charity.

What are you looking for?
Oh, nothing.
You'll find it in the jar where the cookies were.

Dad, could you help me with this homework?
It wouldn't be right.
You could at least try.

Bobby, there were two pieces of cake on the table last night when I went to bed, and this morning there is only one. How do you explain that?

I don't know, Mom. I guess I didn't see the other piece in the dark.

Lady, if you give me a dollar, my brother will imitate a bird for you.
Really, will he whistle like a bird?
No, but he'll eat a worm.

My baby sister gets all the attention in my house.
Why do you say that?
When I bite my fingernails, they yell at me, but when she puts her foot in her mouth, they think it's cute.

Don't be selfish. Let your little brother have the sled half the time.

I do. I let him use it going up hill.

Dad, can I have a bike?
You're too old to be asking for a bike.
I guess you're right. Make it a car.

I always tell my mother everything that happens.
That's nothing. I tell my mother a lot of things that don't happen.

Dad, will you buy me a guitar?
No, you'll be disturbing me with the noise.
I promise to play it only when you're asleep.

Mom, will you change a dime for me?
Sure.
Then change it into a quarter.

There's something wrong with my shaving brush.
That's funny—it was all right yesterday when I painted
   my bike.

Dad, will you help me find the least common
   denominator in this math problem?
Don't tell me it hasn't been found yet—they were
   looking for it when I was a kid!

Why were you kept after school?
Because I didn't know where the Rocky Mountains
   were.
Well, in the future just remember where you put
   things.

Mom, I just saw a dog ten feet high.
I've told you a million times not to exaggerate.

JUL 1 9 1984

9 IDA WILLIAMS

J818.5402
Keller, Charles.
    Oh, brother! Family jokes / compiled
by Charles Keller ; illustrated by
Edward Frascino. -- Englewood Cliffs,
N.J. : Prentice-Hall, c1982.
    46 p. : ill. ; 24 cm.
    Summary: A collection of jokes about
members of the family.
    ISBN 0-13-633305-2

7.95

R00181 44054

    1. Family--Anecdotes, facetiae,
satire, etc. 2. Wit and humor,
Juvenile. I. Frascino, Edward.
II. Title

GA   04 JUN 84   7945012   GAPApc   81-19890r82